Hoopspeak:

*The Xs and Os
of Leading Through
the Language of Basketball*

Julia A. Weaver, MS Ed

Vision Novels

Henderson, NV
2022

Hoopspeak
Julia A. Weaver
Copyright ©2022
All Rights Reserved

Editing: Frances González – Puerto Rico
Book Cover Design: Maxim Babumara - Moldova
Formatting: Vision Novels, Jo A. Wilkins
Additional Cover Work, Richard R Draude

p. cm. — Julia A. Weaver /
Copyright 2022 / Julia A. Weaver

All Rights Reserved

1. Business & Economics / Leadership
2. Self-Help / Motivational & Inspirational
3. Sports & Recreation / Cultural & Social Aspects

ISBN: 978-1-941271-47-6 / Paperback
ISBN: 978-1-941271-65-0 / Paperback

Vision Novels

Printed in USA
1 2 3 4 5 6 7 8 9 0

This book is dedicated to my mother, Margaret Ann Church. She always believed in me and supported me no matter what. She even rode in an old Cadillac with three guys (a radio DJ/women's basketball superfan, a men's basketball player, and a men's soccer player, the last two from the University of North Carolina at Greensboro). They started at midnight to travel over fourteen hours to Memphis, Tennessee, to the South Regional Basketball Tournament to watch me play. She endured Bruce Springsteen on repeat and cigar smoke the entire way. She was that dedicated to supporting me. I know she would be proud of me and this book. I love you, MOM!

Testimonials

"Reading Hoopspeak is more like listening to a podcast than reading a book! The author has written her book in such a way that it feels as if she is talking to you, asking you questions, and making you think.

As a former women's basketball coach, I fell right into the trap. Using basketball terminology to talk about leading people is such a unique and welcoming approach, that I was immediately curious about how the idea would work. It seemed like such a seamless, natural progression, that I quickly forgot I was reading a book about leadership."

Carol Peschel

"This book provides terrific insight into what it takes to be a successful leader. Julia uses a unique and innovative approach to understanding leadership concepts through the language of basketball."

Jacki Silar

Table of Contents

Acknowledgments

I want to thank all my contributors. I asked for your ideas about how basketball and leadership align in your experiences, and you delivered. A little bit of you is here in the book, and I thank you for taking the time to send me your thoughts and ideas.

Jacki Silar, Carol Peschel, Kim Jordan, Paul Damiano, Scott Waterman, Brian Hamilton, Alex Postpischil, Carrie Lasley Ganim, Kacee Reid, Jonathan Hill, Brianne (Dodgen) McCroskey, Chris Holec, Adrian Powell, Frances González, Keri Farley, Lynne Agee, Nelson Bobb, Tom Martin, and Bill.

I would also like to thank my family support system for encouraging me – my sister Susana, niece Sophie, best friend Kim, and dad - Jack.

My sincere appreciation to Jacki, Carol, and Frances for reading the book repeatedly to be sure it made sense, that I wasn't missing any significant pieces, and for reformatting it as often as possible.

Thank you to Sophia Falke @EmbracingGreatness for introducing me to Jo Wilkins at Vision Novels. Networking goes a long way.

And…to all the players, coaches, leaders, and mentors I have connected with along the way. You all inspired me to write this book.

Foreword:
How Basketball Made Me A Fanatical Leader

Why did I write this book? I have knowledge I want to make known to the world. When I think about my life, - basketball, leadership, and coaching have been the common themes throughout my career. I will share what I know, my Xs and Os, regarding leadership through the common language of basketball.

Basketball is a universal language. Everyone, at some level, can understand the terminology. Basketball is inclusive and unbiased. Basketball has no race, sex, gender, or disability. Basketball crosses all socioeconomic lines and can be found on a street corner or court near you in all parts of this diverse world.

The sport of basketball brings people together. In some sense, we all work in teams in our lives, either as a family team (blood or not) or a work team. We interact with people at all levels of our organizations, so why shouldn't we share a common language? If you want to build a powerful culture, you need a common language. Maybe not everyone on your team is a sports enthusiast, but if you are using the language/terms consistently, they will gain another skill by learning the game of basketball.

I have been playing basketball since I was seven years old. I played at recreation centers after school and weekends, in middle school on the school team, in high school on the varsity team even as a ninth-grader, and finally in college. I played in a State Championship in high school and a National Championship at the University of North Carolina at Greensboro. GO SPARTANS! I was a captain and co-captain. I was meant to be a leader. I have experience at all levels of the game of basketball.

I graduated from college and decided I wanted to coach. I left home to follow my dream of coaching. I landed at Cornell University to coach at the Division 1 level. In Ithaca is where I found one of my superpowers. I can analyze situations, see the play as it develops, and strategize to find solutions. This all translates into the leadership world, too. I have been a team leader and a manager in the corporate world. When I left basketball, although it certainly didn't leave me, I always ended up in leadership positions. I have worked in many different industries: education, non-profit, retail, telecommunications, and healthcare. I have started my own businesses. I know basketball and leadership, so I wrote about what I know and love.

When I moved to Ithaca to become an assistant women's basketball coach at Cornell University, I didn't know anyone except for the brief introduction to my fellow staff members and a few people in the athletic community. So, I decided to find my neighborhood basketball court and make my way into "I got next." I thought it would help earn me some respect, make friends, and find my people. I got in the game, and I made friends in the neighborhood who promised to look after me and my space when I was away at games or recruiting. Basketball was our connection, our common language.

I am sure you are wondering how basketball translates into leadership. Allow me to explain. We will introduce basketball terms and how you can use that language to navigate your leadership journey. Basketball terminology aligns with leadership in profound ways. Basketball and leadership have parallel purposes. In both, there is teamwork, team culture, and individual contributors aligning to the overall organizational goals. There is an understanding that everyone doesn't have the same talent level but can play a valuable role, just like the most experienced team member.

This book was written initially with new leaders in mind. However, I am confident that even veteran leaders might identify with the terms and recognize how to use the language of basketball to guide their conversations and interactions. All the ideas and concepts in this book are what I have experienced over my forty-plus years of being a leader and increasing my self-awareness.

My top five strengths have guided me during this book journey. My top strength is Intellection, and authoring this book allowed me to explore the intellectual side of leadership and explain how it relates to basketball. My second and third strengths are Arranger (my superpower to stay organized) and Individualization, which keeps me intrigued with the uniqueness of each person. I am talking directly to you in this book. Lastly, I am fueled by two more strengths, Relater and Deliberative. My Relater strength is powerful as I thrive when working with others. I asked many people for ideas and contributions to this book, which helped me. I am strong at being deliberative. I am careful in my decisions, and you may notice, throughout the book, I will ask a lot of questions to you, the reader, so you can prepare for the challenges of being a leader.

In the past, when I thought I wanted to become a head coach, I started a "philosophy box." It was literally a recipe box filled with note cards. I would use the index cards to write down last-second plays I liked or strategies I picked up while watching other teams or during sessions at the national conventions. I wrote down quotes I wanted to use to keep me motivated. I began to form my own Xs and Os. I encourage you to keep powerful messages and concepts that you want to incorporate when you become a leader or grow as a leader. I also wrote things I didn't want to do as a coach. I would encourage you to do the same. Nowadays, you can keep your notes on a thumb drive, or you can journal. Start your own philosophy box journal. At the end of each quarter, you will find note pages to capture your thoughts, feelings, and actions. This journaling opportunity will serve as YOUR philosophy box.

Companies like to recruit student-athletes because they already have a sense of working on a team and have experience leading in many ways. As a student of the game of basketball, you understand roles and how they fit into the overall success of the team. If you are a basketball player, you will love this book. If you are not, you will learn a lot about basketball, and then you will love this book!

This book is for you if:

- You are a new leader searching for ways to develop your leadership skills.
- You want to use a common language on your team and your organization to build the culture.
- You want to apply basic leadership concepts in your interactions.
- You want to learn more about basketball and how the game relates to leadership concepts.
- You want a book for your book club.
- You want a book that allows you the option to capture your thoughts, feelings, and actions after each quarter.
- You heard about this book from another person, and you can't wait to read it!

Let's embark on this journey together and change the phrase "low hanging fruit" to "fast break"! As I will be posing questions for you to ponder, pause and take the time to write your thoughts, feelings, and actions. If you will accept, a challenge is to think about the opportunities with your team in mind to use your skills

Julia Weaver

and develop your team members into MVPs – Most Valuable People.

When you see this light bulb, you will see a tip, trick, takeaway, or best practice to pay attention to and make a note or two. Add the notes to your own "philosophy box."

Hoopspeak:

*The Xs and Os
of Leading Through
the Language of Basketball*

First Quarter

"Sport is a universal language, building more bridges between people than anything else I can think of."

Sebastian Coe

The Common Language

Shouldn't there be a place where you can learn terminology alongside the strategy so that you can discuss it fluently with others? I think it's essential, and this book is 100% going to do that. This book takes the language of basketball and aligns it with leadership concepts, ideas, examples, and my interpretation of how leadership and basketball come together. Throughout the book, I describe the basketball term and then follow it with an explanation of how it aligns with leading. That's the reason this book is titled Hoopspeak: The Xs and Os of Leading Through the Language of Basketball. It's the strategy behind the terminology. I wanted to create an all-encompassing language that is simple to read and understand. I know basketball, and I have extensive experience as a leader. I share with you the aspiring leader who wants to up your game to reach your highest potential and guide others to do the same. It will be up to you to turn what you learn in this book into action.

Creating a language for things makes it feel more natural. It is the same concept as an inside joke or a silly phrase to make you feel connected. Basketball is a language. Ask any basketball player.

The word teammate will be used to signify anyone you may interact with regardless of their title. Think about how that term might apply to you and your situation. Also, think of these terms as they apply to your team, and all these terms are interchangeable for the purpose of this book.

- Associate/Player – a member of the larger team that may or may not report to you as the leader. The individual contributors that play the game or perform the work in support of the organization.
- Direct Report – a team member that reports directly to you as the leader.
- Colleague/Peer – a team member with whom you work closely. This also may be someone outside of your team or your organization.
- Manager – a role the leader plays to get tasks completed. A manager is more focused on the present.
- Coach – a role the leader plays to develop the players to perform at their best.
- Leader – a role that focuses on development over time. A leader is much more future-focused and looks at the work strategically, not just in the moment.

At any time, you, as a leader, can be in any of these roles. There are times when you must be the player. Get in the game along with your team members. There are times when you have to be a manager to tackle tasks that must get completed for the team's success. You are a coach. You ask questions and probe your team members to help them develop into consistent players and reach the team's overall goals. Furthermore, you are the leader. You are the one the team looks to for guidance. You drive the strategy and bring everyone with you.

Pre-game Warm-up:
Team Norms

"It's not the will to win that matters everyone has that. It's the will to prepare to win that matters."

Paul "Bear" Bryant

Pre-game Warm-up

The pre-game warm-up is the time right before the game, where the team stretches, flexes, and warms up as they are getting ready for a big game. The pre-game in leadership is preparing for your day every day. Start your day with a five-minute huddle to motivate the team and prepare for your day. If you are in sales, set the monetary goal for the day. If you are in retail, acknowledge the sales numbers from the previous day and challenge the team to beat that number. If you are in a call center, recognize team members who had a momentous day or tell the team about some positive feedback you received about the team or an individual. Find places and opportunities to recognize your team. It will go a long way. Another part of the pre-game, before you take the floor and take on a competitor, is to set your expectations. This should happen as soon as you begin to form your team.

When you are forming your team, you and the team should set up team norms. Team norms are a set of operating principles that outline team members' interactions. Norms establish specific and appropriate behavior regarding how the team will work together to accomplish the goals and expectations. Norms help build trust. Trust is critical to the success of any team regardless of the game you are playing.

To create your team norms, ask each member to think of their greatest team experience. Then ask them to propose relevant behaviors based on those great experiences. Capture the behaviors, so everyone can see what is bing proposed. If your team is remote/virtual, use a jam board or whiteboard.

Discuss the recommendations and decide which ones the team is willing to follow as a group. Here are some examples of team norms:

- Start meetings on time, stay on time and end on time.
- Be authentic with each other about ideas, challenges, and feelings.
- Team issues and challenges discussed will be kept in confidence.
- Listen to understand. Ask questions for clarity.
- Participate fully in meetings and training.
- Team members will hold each other accountable for commitments made to one another.
- Limit the use of secondary devices, such as smartphones, personal tablets, and the like, during meetings.

Also, it is imperative to discuss how to respond to a team member who does not follow the team norms. Here are a few key questions to consider:

- What is the process for dealing with a team member that is not honoring the team norms that everyone agreed on?

- How will you influence this process as the leader?

Upon completing the exercise, transfer the "rules of engagement" into a document. Your team may choose to post the list of team norms electronically on a shared site or in YOUR team's "locker room." In the past, I have asked my team members to sign the document electronically or physically. This shows agreement and promotes a sense of camaraderie.

Finally, as new members join your team, introduce the norms early and get their input and buy-in. At times in your scheduled team meetings, you may need to make it a point to discuss what is and what may not be working. Setting team norms are just one of several ways to improve teamwork. This entire book will present you with many ways to enhance individual and team performance, just like the team norms idea.

What are a few challenges
your team might face as a
result of the team norms?

What is your
pre-game message?
Daily? Weekly? Monthly?

Thoughts? Feelings? Actions?

_____

_____

_____

_____

_____

_____

_____

_____

_____

_____

_____

_____

_____

Julia Weaver

_____

_____

_____

_____

_____

_____

_____

_____

_____

_____

_____

_____

_____

_____

_____

Julia Weaver

_____

_____

_____

_____

_____

_____

_____

_____

_____

_____

_____

_____

_____

_____

_____

_____

Team Norm Challenges

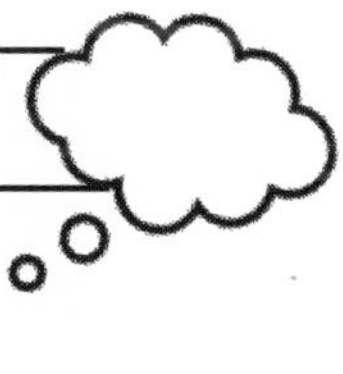

Julia Weaver

_____

_____

_____

_____

_____

_____

_____

_____

_____

_____

_____

_____

_____

_____

_____

_____

Pre-game Messages

Julia Weaver

_____

_____

_____

_____

_____

_____

_____

_____

_____

_____

_____

_____

_____

_____

_____

Second Quarter
Offense: Fifteen Foundational Terms

"Leadership is a contact sport."

Marshall Goldsmith

Offense: Fifteen Foundational Terms

The referee is ready to toss the ball, the jump ball has commenced, and you have first possession. You are on **offense**. The following terms are some of the terms used when a team is on **offense**. Keep in mind these foundational terms below are formal definitions translated into leadership concepts.

1. The Dribble is the action of bouncing the ball with continuous action. **Dribbling** moves you from one place to another. **Dribbling** is one choice from the triple threat position. We will discuss the triple threat later. The **dribble** allows you to move around while still maintaining possession. In leadership, you might "own" the project, and you are **dribbling** around the court/office, searching to add team members to the project. You still have possession; you are just looking for openings, open players, and opportunities.

2. The Shot/Shoot/Shooting is the act of throwing the basketball in the direction of the hoop. Take your **shot**; you miss 100% of the **shots** you don't take. **Shooting** is another possibility from the triple threat position. The **shot** is one way to score solo. The **shot** is something you do. You may have relied on a teammate to pass you the ball, but the **shot** is your own.

Are you ready to take your **shot**, your opportunity?
Do you have the skill and the form?
Are you in your range?
Are you trying a new **shot** you aren't used to taking?

These are great questions to ask yourself before deciding to take the **shot**.

3. A Pass is a way for players to move the ball on the court between teammates. Maybe someone else on the team has an opportunity for a better shot. The **pass** is another option from the triple threat position. In leadership, the **pass** might be when you collaborate with another person. Remember the dribbling around you were doing earlier to find project team members? You found them, and now you are ready to pass them the ball. They can then decide to pass, dribble or shoot.

In basketball, there are several types of passes, but we will only use a few that align to leadership:

4. The Chest Pass is quick, precise, and the most common pass type. As a coach, I always stressed giving your teammate a pass they can catch. It should be an easy pass that will set your teammate up for success. The **chest pass** takes the least time to complete; it is direct and usually a straight line. A **chest pass** may not lead to a score; it is just the act of passing some information or a project to a teammate to continue working on.

5. The Bounce Pass is a pass that goes around the defense or leads your teammate to a shot/opportunity. This pass bounces about two-thirds of the way from the passer to the receiver. When I think of a **bounce pass**, I see it as giving someone a chance for an easy score. They have all the necessary tools they need. They just need you to **pass** the ball so that they can score. Throw them a **bounce pass**!

6. The Skip Pass is a pass that bypasses a person as it goes to another teammate. Can you take a project from A to C instead of in order A, B, C? Can you or did you bypass another team member to make this pass/opportunity? What was your reason for "skipping" a specific person? Do you need to let the person know they have been skipped? How can you develop them so they may not be skipped in the future, and they might get a chest pass or a bounce pass instead?

7. An Assist is attributed to a player who passes the ball to a teammate in a way that leads to a score. In leadership, it might be defined as helping someone achieve a goal or complete a project. It could be

25

an opportunity to allow a team member to expand their knowledge or responsibility. You can set them up for a challenging assignment, but they do the work. You provide support after assessing their skills, challenge them and then offer your support and praise. "An example of an **assist** is when our leaders on the team would often help an associate with difficult customer calls." – Scott Waterman

8. Set a screen; a **screen** is a legal block set by an offensive player on the side of or behind a defender to free a teammate to take a shot or receive a pass. The team member stands between a teammate and the defender and helps your teammate take an open shot or make a strategic move. **A screen** may also be needed if you see a teammate in trouble and feel the need to help. As a leader, you may have to step in and shield your players by absorbing or deflecting a problem from inside and outside the company. It may involve you doing some tedious and meaningless tasks and battling snubs that make life more complicated than necessary for your team members. Great leaders also protect their people from demeaning, overly demanding, and frustrating clients and customers. Also, part of your role as a leader is to protect your people when they screw up. Set that **screen** when they need you.

9. The Give and Go is when a player (A) passes to a teammate (B) and player (A) immediately cuts toward the goal to receive a return pass from a teammate (B). This is a way to reciprocate within your team. The **Give and Go** could be utilized if you chest pass an assignment to a team member, ask them to do the work (delegate), and then get the final product back to deliver it to the organization. Of course, you are giving the teammate credit for the work. Are you expecting something in return when you give assignments or projects? Are your team members honoring the faith you are putting in their ability to do the work AND putting forth the effort to get it done?

10. **The Short Corner** is a strategic offensive area used against zone defenses. The **short corner** is one of my favorite places on the court. In leadership, it could be a unique or secret strategy you might employ to improve a project or an out-of-the-box thought or idea.

11. **The Post Up** is when an offensive player moves down near the basket or into the lower part of the key (the area of the court just below the net, with the outermost border being the free throw line). This offensive player puts their back to the basket and establishes position to receive a pass from a teammate. Get yourself in a position where you can have a quick success. You will most likely require a pass from a teammate to achieve this success or score. How do you establish your position? How do

you **post up** for a score or a positive result from a project?

12. The Fast Break is a quick offensive drive toward the basketball goal while attempting to score before the opponent's defense is set up. You are at an advantage, and you can get a quick score. It is a quick win. You have an advantage on a **fast break**. It is an opportunity to execute a quick and simple shot (lay-up). Ask yourself, is this a **fast break**, do we need to score quickly and increase our momentum, or do we need to stall, stop, and set up our play/project? Do you work the clock? Working the clock means slowing down and working through the process. Maybe you don't need a quick score/win/finish, as this may be detrimental to the overall goal. You can decide; you are the leader.

"I want to challenge you to use the term 'fast break' as the new phrase for 'low hanging fruit.'
Julia A. Weaver

13. The Three-Pointer is a field goal in a basketball game made from beyond the three-point line, a designated arc surrounding the basket. A successful attempt is worth three points, in contrast to the two points awarded for field goals made within the three-point line and the one point for each made free throw.

Steve Jobs suggests a concept of Rule of Three. He says that lists of three things create brief, recognizable patterns. Three is the maximum number of unrelated items that most people can remember after a single exposure. Think about children's books we all are familiar with, The Three Little Pigs or Three Blind Mice.

So, to score a **three-pointer,** keep these in mind. A debriefing strategy (one I have used quite often) that can be used to call for people to think about what they have learned is to ask them:

- What will you START doing because you believe it will help you grow and develop?
- What will you STOP doing because it isn't serving you well?
- What is one thing you will CONTINUE to do because it is going well, and you enjoy doing it?

START. STOP. CONTINUE

To score another **three-pointer**, write bullet points in sets of three (see example above). Do you want to score three more points, give three options for the team to decide about?

14. The Lay-Up is a high-percentage shot that's easier to make. This shot is usually the result of a fast break. In a call center, this might be an easy call that is taken, one that should allow a team member to handle it in a short amount of time. This would help lower an individual's talk time and help them reach their department goals. To enhance a person's confidence, they should be set up to receive some **lay-up** calls. How can you set up a member of your team for a **lay-up**?

15. The Free Throw is an unimpeded attempt at a basket (worth one point) awarded to a player following a foul or other infringement. This is a free shot so take the time to envision it, get into a routine (my routine was three dribbles, spin the ball, bend my knees and shoot). A free throw could be an opportunity for growth, especially after a setback. Set your team members up with a **free throw**, a free and primarily simple shot. They might still miss and not get the point but give them the free shot.

"Leave it out on the court, never quit, make an effort"

Tom Martin by way of Dave Knight

Triple Threat:
Three Crucial Concepts

The triple threat position is undoubtedly the most important start to the offensive process. You have just received a pass; you caught the ball, and now you are in the triple threat position, ready to make some decisions. I heard this cool tidbit when I attended a summit this year. A speaker friend of mine said that we, as humans, make about 35,000 decisions a day. First, I thought, what the heck? 35,000 sounds like an enormous amount of decision-making. I should be exhausted. I looked it up on several reliable sources, and it is true. Therefore, when I think about the triple threat, it is a time where I am going to have to make a calculated decision based on my skill level and confidence.

In my experience and through lots of soul-searching, journaling, and studying, I believe that true leadership falls into three "buckets." See how I used the basketball slang term "bucket" (to score) to talk about leadership. Visible in the graphic, the three "buckets" are:

- Emotional Intelligence
- Engagement
- Execution

Emotional
Intelligence
Engagement
Execution
SCORE

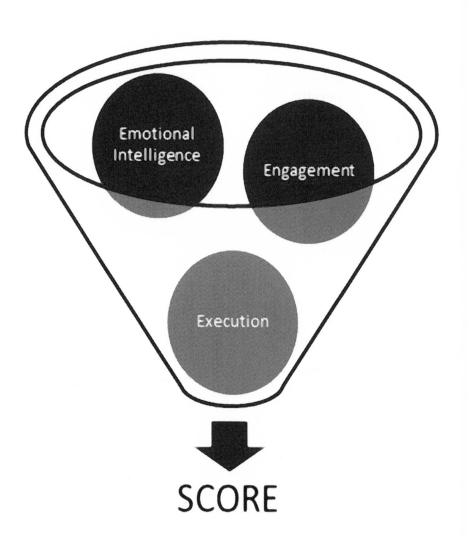

Let me guide you through each one, so you have a better understanding of what they mean:

Emotional Intelligence (EI)

Emotional intelligence is a crucial aspect of a person and is imperative for a leader to become the best they can be. The beautiful thing about emotional intelligence is that it is not fixed. Given the right coach, a good plan, and opportunities, one can enhance their emotional intelligence. Please keep in mind that there are books written on emotional intelligence. I am just offering a small piece of what it means to be emotionally intelligent because it is necessary to be effective.

In its simplest form, emotional intelligence is broken down into four major components.

Self-Awareness	Self-Management
Social Awareness	Relationship Management

Take an Emotional Intelligence assessment. Learn more about how to do that in the last chapter.

The first component is **Self-Awareness,** and it's about how your emotions impact you and others. To have a high level of self-awareness, you have a keen understanding of how your emotions might be helping or hindering your performance. You are the one who knows what you are feeling and why. In being more self-aware, you also understand how to recognize your triggers. Those with a powerful sense of self-awareness know their strengths and limitations and are truly clear about their values. If you recall, I mentioned that I was self-aware of my strengths, superpowers, and how they drive me. I am clear about them, which has helped me be a better leader. Successful leaders have a heightened level of self-awareness; they understand themselves, their behaviors, and actions, and how those behaviors and actions are interpreted by and directly impact those they lead. I also believe that you can't be self-aware if you aren't vulnerable.

As a leader, you need to understand that being vulnerable is not weak or bleak. Vulnerability allows team members to feel more open and honest with their fears, questions, mistakes, and barriers, providing stronger team connection and performance. For reference, I invite you to check out Brene Brown's TEDTalk about vulnerability. Two of my takeaways from her wisdom: "Leaders and not just the brave ones, need to be courageous, self-aware, and concerned with doing the right things." and "We can measure how brave you are by how vulnerable you're willing to be."

Questions to ask yourself to gauge your **Self-Awareness**:

- Am I being true to myself?
- What, if anything, do I need to change about myself to be more effective as a

leader?

- Can I accurately describe the impact I have on others emotionally?
- What situations make me feel terrible, and what do they have in common?
- What actions could trigger emotions in me?

To improve your **Self-Awareness**, try the following:

- Make conscious choices.
- Be aware of how your body is reacting. Do you sweat? Is your face red and heating up? Are you experiencing a fight or flight sensation (anxiety)?
- Know your triggers. Does someone crying trigger you? Does a perceived "lazy," unmotivated person who just comes to work to get paid and not show any ambition trigger you? Do you avoid a talker, a non-talker, or the office clown?
- Know your strengths and areas of development (limitations).
- Don't judge your feelings; accept them as they are and where you are.

The second component of emotional intelligence is **Self-Management**, and it involves your ability to control and have a conscious attitude towards your feelings, actions, and behaviors. In its simplest form, it is the ability to manage self. A few fundamental self-management skills include communication skills, people skills, stress management techniques, anger management, and time management strategies.

Ask these questions to gauge your **Self-Management** skills:

- What are you doing to manage yourself and your emotions?
- Are you acting in healthy ways, and are you adaptable?
- Do you maintain a positive outlook even on the tough days?
- What activities are you doing when you feel a negative emotion creeping up? Yoga? Taking a walk? Taking deep breaths?
- What do you do when you are triggered?

 To improve **Self-Management**, try the following:

- Journal or self-talk.
- Relieve stress by being active in some way or getting a massage.
- Meditate as often as you can.
- Communicate, don't hold on to the feelings.

The third component is **Social Awareness**, and it can be described as the ability to recognize and understand the moods of others and groups. Social awareness is the ability to detect crucial networks and nuances at work in an organization. It is in the ability to read a room, notice body language and facial expressions, or in the virtual world, be aware of the emojis people might be sharing? A keen social awareness lies in your ability to know the "temperature" of the zoom room. It is more complex because people can hide, but it is crucial to leading a virtual team.

It is essential to see the big picture, or you may need to zoom in at times. As a leader, you must know when to use each viewpoint. For example, are you thrilled about a new project because you have had time to think it through, but they are not as enthusiastic when you present it to the team? What could you have done differently to share the news? Should you be zoomed in or zoomed out? Another example is that the team is coming off an emotional high after completing a big project with lofty expectations. Now you must tell them the project lost money and is being discontinued. What will you do? How will being socially aware help in this situation?

To gauge your **Social Awareness**, here are some questions to guide you:

- What have you done lately to build a stronger relationship with any of your team members? What was the result?
- Can you recall a time when someone felt you were unfair? What did you do? What

would you do differently?

- Is your current work environment a good cultural fit for you?
- What are some things you can do to be an active listener?
- What can you learn by understanding the perspectives of others?

To improve your **Social Awareness**, try the following:

- Listen more and listen with your heart so you can empathize if needed.
- Be present. Notice the details.
- Ask your team members about themselves and—this is important—listen to what they tell you.
- Think about ways to collaborate with colleagues and employees. How can you actively contribute?
- Learn to think about how you can help the team, not how they can help you.

Relationship Management is the final component and is about using your awareness to manage your interactions with others. This competency focuses on inspiring others, creating resonance to a company's mission or vision, challenging the status quo, and bringing out differing perspectives in a collaborative fashion. To manage your relationships effectively, you can even build relationships with those you may not have a good relationship with. You use empathy when coaching if you are efficient at managing relationships.

To gauge your **Relationship Management** skills, ask these questions of yourself:

- Do people in your circle of trust look like you? How can you broaden your circle?
- How diverse is your team?
- On an average day, is your main focus on results and tasks or people and emotions?
- How did you find common ground with someone you may not agree with or have a good relationship with?
- Think about a time you failed to establish or maintain a relationship with a peer. What could you do differently next time?

To improve in **Relationship Management**, try the following:

- Be direct without emotional attachment.
- Build trust with those around you.
- Acknowledge where the other person is, meet them where they are.
- Ask questions.
- Use more praise.

As we conclude the section on emotional intelligence, strengths overdone can become areas of opportunity just like anything else. If you have high emotional intelligence, there are potential implications:

- Your creativity may be decreased.
- You might have difficulty giving and receiving negative feedback.
- You might be reluctant to ruffle feathers and challenge the status quo.
- You may not take as many risks.

If you have low emotional intelligence, these may be some signs to be aware of:

- You hide your feelings because you think feelings and emotions don't belong at work.
- You may be very argumentative on multiple topics in both individual and team meetings
- You may tend to blame others.
- You may be insensitive to the feelings and thoughts of others.
- You are focused on yourself, aka the "what about me?" Syndrome.

Before we move to the other triple threats of leadership, I want to take a deeper dive into empathy. Being empathetic is essential and lies within two EI components, **Social Awareness and Relationship Management**. Empathy is an important skill to develop to be a truly, emotionally intelligent leader. If you want to be socially aware and build strong relationships across your organization, you will need to be empathetic. In my leader life, I have heard people say that emotions don't belong at work. Guess what? Emotions are entrenched in your organization and your team, and the better you can acknowledge and respond to the emotions, the better leader you will be, I promise.

Empathy means taking the perspective of others. I have used this example in some of the workshops I have delivered to explain empathy simply. Look at the picture below as I explain how I view empathy. If you are looking at the fishbowl, the empty one is the "perspective of others." You can see the one fish is ready and willing to jump in the bowl with the "perspective of others."

The fish is not just staying in the other bowl looking at the empty bowl and saying or thinking – "Yeah, I understand that." Only saying you understand is considered a statement of sympathy, not empathy. You are just acknowledging the feeling, not willing to get in the fishbowl. You are just looking into "the perspective of others" – even standing in judgment of it.

In our example, empathy is the willingness to get in the bowl with another person or fish. You express that you understand because you are now in the bowl with them. To be empathetic, you are not only saying "I understand," but you are also saying, "it is tough to make momentous changes; let me get in there with you and share in your feelings/emotions." Even if you haven't experienced the exact issue/tragedy/change as the person, you are in there with them and willing to listen. You could even say, "I don't know what it feels like to make a substantial change, yet I am glad you told me." To show empathy, ask yourself, are you willing to jump into the fishbowl with others, or would you rather just stay outside the bowl or in your bowl? What are you willing to do? Are you ready to be vulnerable too? Remember that being vulnerable builds connections and can elevate team performance.

To create the conditions for engagement, pride, and performance, outstanding leadership takes a perfect blend of all kinds of skills. What skill tops the list of what leaders must get right to be successful - Empathy. To be empathetic means you will need to connect with all the players on your team, which leads us to our next triple threat concept, Engagement.

Engagement

Engagement is a huge part of good leadership, and it is another concept of the **triple threat**. It's critical to understand what we mean when saying "engagement." The degree of energy experienced is a combination of how you perceive changes (self-awareness), what's going on around you (social awareness), and how engaged you are. As a result, highly engaged people have a favorable impression of the changes around them, and they devote more energy to their work and other activities.

People have the option of being engaged or not. As a dedicated leader, your job is to create the circumstances in which they choose to participate. It might not be as challenging for them to accept your assistance in the right conditions. Before you can help, it's essential to understand your employees' perspectives in various situations. Many studies focus on why people leave an organization; more importantly, what happens if they decide to stay. How will you keep your team engaged?

A perfect example of engaging and a pre-game

experience involves the actions of a middle school principal in the heart of the District of Columbia – Shaw area. My best friend, Brian K. Betts, waited outside in the rain, sleet, snow, and sun for every student to arrive at school. He greeted every student every single day of the week. Without fail, he was there to make them feel important to him and the school and offered them the opportunity to engage. He welcomed them with high fives, handshakes, fist bumps, and words of encouragement. They were excited to be there because he made them feel valued. They wanted to engage with him, with each other, and in the classroom. Attendance records in his school were broken each year. May he rest in peace knowing he made a difference in those kids' lives.

When you think about your team, here are some questions your employees may be asking themselves as they decide whether to engage or not:

- Why should I get excited about work?
- What do my leaders and mentors expect of me?
- Am I in an organizational team culture that cares about me?
- How will I know how I am doing?
- How do I work effectively with others?
- Is leadership displaying a positive example and being a good role model?

As the leader, it is your responsibility to know the answers and set the tone for engagement. It's not a new notion that there's a link between employee engagement and organizational performance. A good number of organizations have adopted engagement as a practice, and most have launched various employee resource groups or ERGs to drive associate engagement in the workplace.

In my opinion, engagement is one of the critical factors to a team's success. As a result, it is one of the triple threats of leader development. Now that we are experiencing a remote and virtual reality, engagement is more important than ever.

The three other most widely cited factors affecting employee engagement and experience are, according to *HR.com*:

- A positive culture with no or few toxic behaviors – building a culture of positivity is vital.
- Trust in leaders through engaging team members and providing opportunities for those team members.
- Having a voice that's listened to with emotional intelligence, as discussed previously.

Another *HR.com* study, "The State of Employee Engagement," found that 81% consider trust in leaders to be the most crucial factor impacting employee engagement, followed closely by an employee's immediate relationship with their supervisor. However, only 29% of all HR professionals say their organizations have leaders who prioritize engagement. The third most highly rated factor—having a voice that's listened to—is another area of concern in today's organizations. HR.com's research on engagement shows that many of today's leaders tend to lack good employee listening skills. This is a part of emotional intelligence and if you engage, take the time to truly listen to your team members. Listen for new insights and new ways of thinking.

In my playing days, our head coach tasked each of us to do the pre-game message, whether a poem, a parable, a quote, or a song. One of my teammates made a joke and said, "Can you hear me in the back?" It made all of us laugh, but it is true; you must hear what people are saying, even if they are in the back, and truly listen. There is a logical reason we have two ears and one mouth.

Over half of respondents in the previously mentioned HR study associate two statements with engagement: "employees' willingness to give their best at work" and "employees' commitment to the organization and its objectives."

What are you currently doing to get your team engaged? Being engaged or disengaged is one aspect of the entire employee experience and is affected by factors such as personal and professional development, culture (team culture), and exceptional leadership. A winning culture coupled with excellent leadership can help you win titles, not just a few games.

There is some truth to the saying, "no one leaves a job; they leave a boss." I have left organizations and jobs due to a poor relationship with a boss. Every moment a leader spends with employees can make a critical difference in their experience. Outstanding leadership is not easy because it could take a dozen positive interactions to make up for one bad one. Of course, leadership requires coaching, empathy, collaboration, and many other skills. Still, a leader should help employees find meaning in their work, connect the individual values to the organization, and create a sense of purpose.

When focusing on engagement, it's essential to understand who is ready to engage and who may need a nudge to move ahead. You must create opportunities for all members of the team to engage! Strategic leaders live in the future by concentrating on trends and financial goals six, nine, and twelve months out. They are looking at the next quarter's goals. Team members/players primarily function in the present and concentrate on completing significant daily deliverables. Many players/associates find it difficult to shift into the mindset of future strategy and need time to process. Through engaging conversations during your one on ones, you can gauge where your team members are in the process of change as it occurs on your team and within the organization. This one-on-one time provides you with another opportunity to actively listen.

By placing yourself in your employees' shoes (the fishbowl of perspective of others), you are better prepared to help them move toward being committed to the goals and engaged. According to an article by Tom Roth, *Engagement Starts with Your Leaders: Create a Culture of High Energy and Commitment Through the 4 Levels of Leadership*, he suggests three steps you can take today to become the leader you want to be:

- Demonstrate a clear commitment to your leadership purpose and values. Walk your talk!
- Be a positive role model for the beliefs, practices, customs, and behaviors you want all employees to exhibit in their interactions with one another and their day-to-day work. Walk your talk!
- Encourage all employees to understand and share those same beliefs and behaviors, and coach to them. Walk your talk!

The team's culture will happen whether you influence it or not as you move your team forward today. Ask yourself these questions:

- Are you and your leaders actively involved in establishing a culture of engagement? If not, they need to be, with you setting the example.
- Are you setting your players up for success by making chest passes and bounce passes (recording an assist)?

"A leader's job is to develop committed followers. Bad leaders destroy their followers' sense of commitment."

Dean Smith

 Find fifteen tips for engaging your team in the Overtime section.

Execution

Execution is the final concept in the triple threat model. Execution is about performing at the highest level through the vision, the mission, and doing what you say you will do (walking the talk). Execution is about directing the plan or the strategy, the Xs and Os, that you or your organization has decided to implement. To execute at the highest level, the leader must have a strategic mindset and the skills to accomplish the

49

goals. A true team leader will bring everyone with you, and it will take all the things we have discussed so far, including emotional intelligence and engagement.

Effective execution will only be feasible if you hold your team accountable, set clear expectations, and provide the team members' tools to be successful. Hold team meetings to keep the team updated on milestones and challenges. Meet individually with the players that are involved in the organizational projects. Be consistent with your one on ones. Ideally, it would be best to meet with your team members weekly. If not weekly, then bi-weekly.

You may have to call some **timeouts**. You may encounter some **fouls**. We will discuss these terms later. You will have to decide whether to **pass, dribble or shoot** out of the triple threat position.

When a leader's words and actions sync, team members will trust them more and feel more engaged and committed. People may not remember what you say, but they will remember how you made them feel, as the saying goes.

Starting with the triple threat position and thinking about emotional intelligence, engagement, and execution: Will you **pass** – collaborate? Will you **shoot**, take a risk, and execute on your own? Will you **dribble**? Take it in a different direction and work with someone else, take it to the basket yourself, or **give and go** (reciprocate)?

We have covered a lot in the first two quarters, team norms, fifteen fundamental terms, and the especially important triple threat. Now is a great time to PAUSE and write your thoughts, feelings, and actions. The clock has run down, and it is Halftime.

Which current projects can
you pass to a team member
to record an assist?

You need to deliver an
important message to the team—
Shoot a three pointer

Who can you make a
bounce pass to so they
can score a lay-up?

How can you take advantage
of a triple threat option

Record an Assist

_____

_____

_____

_____

_____

_____

_____

_____

_____

_____

_____

_____

Julia Weaver

_____

_____

_____

_____

_____

_____

_____

_____

_____

_____

_____

_____

_____

_____

_____

Shoot A Three Pointer

Julia Weaver

Bounce Pass

Triple Threat Option

_____

_____

_____

_____

_____

_____

_____

_____

_____

_____

_____

_____

_____

Julia Weaver

_____

_____

_____

_____

_____

_____

_____

_____

_____

_____

_____

_____

_____

_____

_____

_____

_____

_____

_____

_____

_____

_____

_____

_____

_____

_____

_____

_____

_____

_____

_____

_____

Julia Weaver

Halftime

Even the simplest tools can empower people to do great things.

Biz Stone

Halftime

Halftime comes for a reason and allows time for the team to adjust. This can be in an all-team meeting or a meeting among the team leaders. The leaders may huddle first to identify the message and then bring the team in to discuss a plan, not just "tell." Remember, you are trying to establish a culture of engagement.

Your halftime speech may be during a larger team meeting where the goals may have to shift. Are you behind and need to pick up the pace? Do you need to chip away, knocking out one challenge at a time? Do you need to set up a full-court press? Or are you in the lead, and you just need to tweak some things? Maybe it is just a need to keep the momentum going?

The strategy hasn't changed; you just may need to make some adjustments. The third and fourth quarters will add even more tools to your toolkit.

Find an opportunity
for a Give and Go

Start a Fast Break and get
a quick score (success)

Make a skip pass to a team
member or leader this week

Set up a team member to
shoot a free throw today

In what situation did you express
empathy this week? How did it go?

What could you do
differently the next time?

In your team meetings lately,
what did you notice about
the team atmosphere?

Give and Go's

Julia Weaver

Fast Breaks

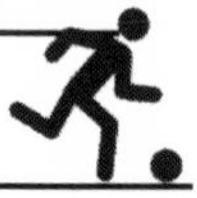

Free Throws

_____

_____

_____

_____

_____

_____

_____

_____

_____

_____

_____

_____

_____

_____

Julia Weaver

_____

_____

_____

_____

_____

_____

_____

_____

_____

_____

_____

_____

_____

_____

_____

_____

_____

Expressions of Empathy

Julia Weaver

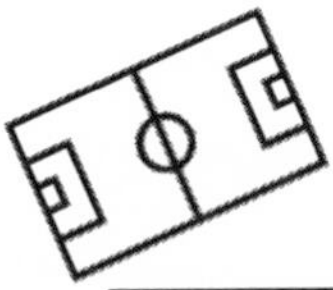

Julia Weaver

Team Atmosphere

Julia Weaver

_____

_____

_____

_____

_____

_____

_____

_____

_____

_____

_____

_____

_____

_____

_____

_____

Third Quarter
Defense: Six Successful Strategies

"Effective teamwork begins and ends with communication."

Coach K

Defense

Defense is defined around strategies, alignment, and positioning to keep the opposing team from scoring. In leadership, we are not genuinely trying to stop someone, but there are many principles about defense that do align with leadership:

    1. Person to person or player to player defense is a defensive formation where each player is assigned a specific offensive player to follow and defend on the court. **Player to player defense** might be in the form of mentoring or using a buddy system during on-boarding. A player is assigned to another player to help them transition onto the team.

    2. The Zone is a system of defense in which each player guards an assigned area rather than a specified opponent/player. This might look like a team project, event, or leadership or team building meeting. All the team is working together.

Defense has many different looks and alignment, like a 2:3 zone, a 1:3:1 **zone,** or a match-up **zone,** but for our purposes, we will just stay with thinking in terms of a basic zone or a player-to-player defensive alignment. Something that you are always in control of, no matter how skilled you are or how well you are leading, is your energy and effort. Your energy level and ability to effectively communicate are the keys to any defense and being a great leader and mentor.

Communication is a skill that any player or leader can be good at because it only takes deciding to do it. The best defensive teams in basketball are filled with players working together to get the job/project accomplished. This only happens, though, if each player communicates their responsibility in a way that their teammates can trust them to be where they need to be. There are many moving parts on defense, so the better you can communicate what you are doing, the easier it will be for your teammates. This happens in a **player-to-player defense** and a **zone defense**. Your communication will also let your teammates know what they need to do in any situation.

One of the main reasons work does not get accomplished is that the entire team is sometimes not informed or on the same page as the rest of the team. This is most likely due to a lack of communication. Think about getting into a zone defense and talking to each other constantly. Apply that concept to your team interactions. Be in constant communication with teammates to help prevent defensive breakdowns.

Anticipating vs. Reacting:

- Be aware of what is going on around you. Anticipate the next move.
- If you constantly react to the ball or the situation, you will get beat.

I challenge you to think back to a time when you avoided making a significant decision because of how you thought it would be received. At the moment, you may have thought it was a good decision because those around you would be pleased. However, all it did was isolate you and cause more damage to the team and the organization.

I found a couple of examples of leadership in a sport setting from the Ted Lasso series on Netflix. This is an instance where Ted stands out. He is willing to make decisions that he believes are best for the team, even if it frustrates everyone else. When Jamie, their star player, refuses to pass the ball, Ted benches him. This decision angers an entire stadium of fans, but Ted knew it was the right thing to do for the club's sake. Remember, great leaders, do the right thing. What decisions are you making for the good of the team or the organization, even if it is not a popular decision?

A former colleague of mine at The Center for Creative Leadership, Paul Damiano, offered this impressive tidbit about leadership and the **screen switch**, which is a tactic in **player-to-player** defense.

When playing defense, deciding whether to "switch" (or not) when an opposing offensive player sets a pick for their teammate. The metaphor for leadership has to do with overall team agility, knowing your team and your opponent's strengths, and having good situational awareness. For example, if you and your defensive teammate choose not to switch, you might get screened too easily and give up an open or easy shot opportunity. However, if you do switch, this could cause a potential mismatch in favor of the offense. So, the agility comes from knowing when to switch and then whether to go over or under a screen. This decision should be made fluidly and agilely depending on a number of variables (e.g., opponents involved in the pick, time left on the shot clock, time left in the game, offensive player's abilities, defensive player abilities, number of fouls left to give, position on the floor, etc.). The leader (coach) or lead players on the floor need to have a good "in-the-moment" awareness of these variables and then decide accordingly. And some of these decisions may actually be short-term/sub-optimal (like a point guard switching and now finding themselves guarding the opposing team's center). But the leader must decide to take a temporary short-term disadvantage in hopes that the larger strategy and vision will prevail. Only a leader with good situational awareness, decisional agility, and having a larger vision will be able to make these many decisions effectively throughout the course of the game.

As we continue our defensive path, there are a few terms that belong in the defense section that we have not mentioned yet:

3. A Rebound is when a player retrieves the ball after a missed field goal attempt. This happens when you might fail or if you miss a shot or opportunity. You must **rebound**.

A **rebound** example might be after you had a troublesome experience. Did you get the **rebound** and get a second chance, or did the defense get it, and you lose possession of the opportunity?

A **rebound** in leadership might be needed when a person mismanages a project. How will they **rebound** or correct it for the next time? If you lose an account or a deal fell through, ask yourself these questions:

- Did you give your best effort?
- Were you fully tuned into the project or the pitch mentally?
- Did you have all the tools to be successful?
- What could you have done better if you could do it again?
- Challenge yourself with the Start, Stop, Continue strategy tool.

4. The Hedge and Recover is when the defender who is guarding the offensive player who sets the screen jumps out higher than their defenders or "hedges" the ball. The **hedge** from your teammate gives the defender time to recover and stay with the ball handler. To hedge is to step in front of the dribbler to stop progress. A **hedge** is meant to temporarily help your teammate, so you then need to retreat or recover and get back to your job.

Yes, I know a **hedge** is usually to help your teammate, but, in this case, let's think of a **hedge** as perhaps you or another teammate are getting in the way. How are you hedging your teammates? Are you getting in the way of forward progress for your teammates or direct reports?

5. The Jump ball happens when two opposing players try to gain control of the ball, and they get "tied up." Have you given your team too much work, so they feel they are stuck? Initiate a jump ball. Figuratively, line them up in the middle and divide the work equitably. One may "win" the jump and get more work, so reward that as if they get a chance to be on offense now, after winning the **"jump ball."**

6. The Box Out means to position oneself between an opposing player and the basket to hinder the opposing player from rebounding or tipping in a shot, also known as a block out. As a leader, you may need to protect the team. Take care of the team by advocating, which could mean taking a hit publicly, **boxing out** the outside negative influences.

Let's discuss a **full-court press** since it might be a possibility to consider. A **full-court press** is usually applied when you are trying to pick up momentum, get a quick turnover, surprise the offense, or when you are behind and need to catch up. A **full-court press** aims to create offense out of defensive formation. Being behind in the game or a project will link it to leadership.

A friend shared a situation that certainly struck me as needing a **full-court press**. The situation involved a company that is a large Fortune 500 corporation headquartered in New York City. It was September 12th, 2001, chaos followed, and every person in the corporation had to get into **full-court press** mode. "What should we do," they were asking each other? Our clients, consumers, and people have been highly affected by the tragedy in the US, and we probably need to call a **timeout** and **rebound**. We are already behind and against the clock in this tumultuous situation. It is most definitely an "all hands on deck" situation, and we must focus on our customers and our accounts in the New York City area. Every account representative will need to immediately reach out to those accounts in New York City and ensure them that we are supporting them any way we can. Like the full-court press, we will create offense from a defensive strategy.

The On the Court Culture:
Four Concepts to Elevate Your Game

"Luck has nothing to do with it because I have spent many, many hours, countless hours, on the court working for my one moment in time, not knowing when it would come."

Serena Williams

Court Culture

You are on the court and within the boundaries of your area/department within the organization. Being on the court is about being with your team and ready to play the game. You are prepared to take on the opponents/competition because your team is prepared and with you. Just to give you some data, you might want to know that a basketball court, end line, and sideline is 94' x 50'. The connection to leadership is to lead your team within your 94'x 50', your department, or unit within the organization.

When you step on the court, you may be in the midst of your project, at the heart of a new launch, or administering a new process. Let's discuss some of the on the court terms that take place within your team:

    1. A Timeout is a halt in play on the court. It might look like a quick check-in or a team huddle. You might need to call a timeout to make an adjustment or prevent the team or project from derailing.

 Don't be afraid of taking a timeout.

And by all means, do not save those timeouts! Why are you saving them? They don't all add up at the end of the year. There is no carryover from day to day, week to week, or year to year. Please resist the urge only to call timeouts when it's going bad. A **timeout** is not always to stop derailing; sometimes, you need to call a **timeout** to rest your people and regroup. I love the idea of a well-executed **timeout**! Momentum is a remarkable thing (especially when you have it). Conversely, it can ruin a well-executed plan when you don't have that momentum.

"Whether in business, my own life, or dealing with the kids...a well-executed **timeout** *has helped tremendously."*
Jonathan Hill

A well-executed timeout gives a leader time to think, it gives you time to not let emotions get in the way, and it gives you time to consider an alternate plan. Take a moment to consider what is going on with your team today, right now, as you are reading this. Do you need to call a **timeout**? Are your players weary from working diligently on a project? Are they trying to meet unreasonable deadlines? Do you need to stop and celebrate some positive accomplishments or met milestones? Do you need to recognize a player or multiple players for work well done?

Catch your team members doing something right!

Here is a real-life example by Alex Postpischil about when the leader saw a need to call a **timeout**:

When I'm seeing a process that isn't quite working as planned - let's take a **timeout**: assess what's happening, recall what our goal is, and how we should adjust the process to achieve the goal. This has happened many times as I was building scenery for a show, and something didn't quite fit. One example is when I was working at The Washington Opera, and we were installing an upstage wall for "Turandot." The notes from the earlier performances (about a decade prior) said to use certain sizes of scaffolding to build the wall. When we reached the top level and started to hang the scenery, it turned out the scaffolding was too short. **Timeout**! We measured, determined the correct size scaffolding needed, took the wall down, and rebuilt it with the correct size scaffolding. I also updated the notes for the production so the next time the opera was produced, the crew would have the correct information. This example could also fall into the **rebound** category since we recovered from the mistake after the timeout and made corrections.

A leader would need to call a **timeout** when talking to an individual or a group, and the conversation is quickly going downhill or in a nonproductive manner. All parties would just need a mental break to reset and regroup. A good coach knows when to call a **timeout**, calm the team down and design a new strategy to counteract the current problem. It doesn't end there. One way may work, while another fails. It's up to the team leader to continually adjust and stay ahead of the competition or the project.

Mistakes happen in the workplace and on the basketball court, and a good leader will call a **timeout** and refocus the team by establishing a culture centered on accountability.

   2. A Turnover occurs when a team loses possession of the ball. We are using this term in the truest sense. Are you losing possession of your people? Those very people that you have invested time and money into. What is happening in the organization right now? Why are people leaving? What might you be contributing to the **turnover** issue? It could be your fault. You could normalize mistakes. What are the lessons learned as mistakes are made? If a team member is continually making mistakes, pull that person aside, similar to when you make a substitution. Talk to that team member on the bench/in your office. Offer feedback on how the behavior affects the team, the customers, and the organization. Keep building that culture of accountability. Is your organization experiencing lots of turnovers? You need to ask the hard question – why!

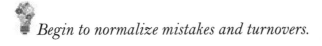

Begin to normalize mistakes and turnovers.

A mistake is a common event in the game of basketball. It happens all the time. Good shooters miss shots just like good employees miss deadlines. Good passers toss the ball off a teammate's leg or throw it out of bounds like good employees fumble during a presentation. Good defenders get beaten to the ball like good employees forget to send an email update. Since it happens to everyone in every game, it hardly seems like a cause for getting upset and hanging your head. If a mistake is made, make a swift transition, call a timeout if you need it and do your best under the circumstances.

3.   **The Pivot** in basketball is an action the ball-handler can take by rotating around a pivot foot without picking it up. Move yourself or the team in a different direction if what you are currently doing is not working. Your people can't get open because they don't have the bandwidth, or they don't have the appropriate skills. Pivot until you can decide if you can make a **pass** or **dribble** around without doing further damage?

4.   **A Foul** is an infraction of the rules more serious than just a violation or a turnover. **Fouls** are categorized as offensive or defensive and are broken down into **personal, technical,** and **flagrant fouls**. Each player is only given five fouls before being disqualified from the game. If you or a team member is acquiring five fouls or more, it might be time for you to evaluate what is going on. If five fouls are awarded before the game ends, this is known as 'fouling out.' It might be time for you to make some changes, either personally or on your team, if people are "fouling out."

- **<u>A Personal Foul</u>** is a breach of the rules against a player.
- **<u>A Technical Foul</u>** is given to a player on the court, a player on the bench, or even the coach if they act out of control. For the most part, a technical foul results from unsportsmanlike conduct expressed during the game. Sometimes technical fouls are intentional to get the attention of a cause, a person, or a project. I am not saying to do anything unethical, but sometimes you must make some noise to get noticed. Especially if you are trying to change the culture or shake things up and challenge the status quo.
- **<u>A Flagrant Foul</u>** is not one you want to get. Flagrant fouls are considered excessive, unnecessary, or intentional. This may be an unethical move or not supportive of the organization, your team, or you. A flagrant foul may violate your own or a team members' values. Ask yourself if what is taking place

violates a value that you or someone else may have. It might be obvious.

As I was developing my philosophy about the kind of coach I wanted to be, I did aspire to be a head coach; I also kept a list of things I did not want to do as a coach. One of those things was being known as someone who makes a **flagrant foul**. It is just as beneficial to know what kind of leader you don't want to be because it has affected you negatively in some way. You don't want to make the same mistake, don't relive the situation. You have the power to change the narrative if that situation comes up for you as a leader. My advice is to stay clear of flagrant fouls. What would you do differently so it is not a flagrant foul? How will doing it differently change the outcome for you, the team, or the organization? Below are some real examples of fouls; what kind do you think they are, personal, technical, or flagrant?

1st Foul - Theatre is a collaborative process. The most common foul is when design and production changes are made outside of the regular design/ production meetings that usually occur weekly. While the creative process can be inspired at any time, the foul occurs when those changes are not communicated to the rest of the staff.

2nd Foul - When a person in a leadership position doesn't practice what they preach. Example: As a leader, you are expected to be on time each day, and you constantly show up late to work or for meetings.

3rd Foul - Taking credit for another team member's success or performance.

4th Foul - A leader was overheard saying that they wished Human Resources had told them that the veteran they hired had Post Traumatic Stress Disorder (PTSD) and that the person may have a cognitive delay. The leader expressed to others on the team that they wouldn't have hired the person if they had known that information.

5th Foul - A leader adamantly states that people who take FMLA (Family Medical Leave Act) are working the system. Then that person they were telling, indeed, must take FMLA to take care of their mental health. The employee feels rejected, disrespected, and has an overall sense of not being supported. They are not working the system, but the belief is out there.

Be aware if you, the team, or the organization continually commit fouls. There may be something happening that is more serious and certainly deserves your attention. Fouls are red flags.

If you and your team can talk productively about fouls, you will develop trust within the team and elevate your game.

In what ways did a team
member rebound this week?

Can you identify a reason why you
might need to pivot this week?

How have you enhanced
your communication skills?

What is one of your strengths? How
can you use that strength this week?

Rebounds?

_____

_____

_____

_____

_____

_____

_____

_____

_____

_____

_____

_____

_____

_____

_____

Pivots of the week?

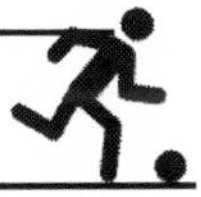

Communication Skills

Strengths?

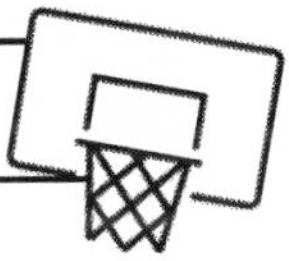

Julia Weaver

Have you committed any
fouls this week?

If so, was it—
Personal? Technical? Flagrant?

Has anyone on your team committed
any fouls this week?
Personal? Technical? Flagrant?

How did it impact the team?

Fouls

_____

_____

_____

_____

_____

_____

_____

_____

_____

_____

_____

_____

_____

_____

_____

Julia Weaver

Personal? Technical? Flagrant?

_____

_____

_____

_____

_____

_____

_____

_____

_____

_____

_____

_____

_____

_____

Team Impact

_____

_____

_____

_____

_____

_____

_____

_____

_____

_____

_____

_____

_____

_____

_____

Do you need to call any
timeouts this week?

If so, in what situation?

What will you do to
change the narrative?

Timeouts?

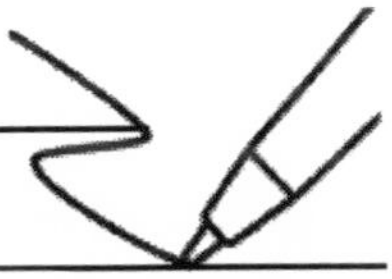

Julia Weaver

_____

_____

_____

_____

_____

_____

_____

_____

_____

_____

_____

_____

_____

_____

Fourth Quarter
Building the Team:
Build Your Bench Strength and Recruiting

"I am convinced that nothing we do is more important than hiring and developing people. At the end of the day, you bet on people, not on strategies."

Lawrence Bossidy, GE

Building Your Team

Building your team may be one of the most important responsibilities you have as a leader. High-performing teams make a tremendous impact on an organization. Just like in any game, the goal is to "win" the game so you can win championships. You win a bid or a proposal so you can be the best of the best in your field. Teams that compete at that level must be high-performing consistently, and they all go through various stages of development. In business, you will want to build your team because, as a team is how you will accomplish organizational goals. As a leader, you have the opportunity to build your team the way you want. It takes work to get to the high-performing stage, but you can do it with emotional intelligence, engagement, communication, opportunities, and execution.

Psychologist Bruce Tuckman produced the memorable phrase "forming, storming, norming and performing" in his 1965 paper, "Developmental Sequence in Small Groups." It's still relevant today when we talk about teams and how they develop into high-performing. As a leader, you will need to understand how the team develops, so you know how to help move them through the stages. Let's introduce all the stages and then discuss how you, as the leader, can keep the team moving forward.

Forming is one of the stages of Tuckman's model of team development. Forming usually happens when a new team is forming. However, you can be in forming if you make changes to a team, add team members, or add an entirely new team. In this stage, there is an opportunity to communicate about the team's mission and vision. During this stage, there will be a lot of curiosity, anxiousness, and excitement within the team. The team is just getting to know each other. This stage is critical because it does set the stage for the course of the team and how they will work together to accomplish the goals. This is a time for you to be very present with the team as the leader. The team is not high performing during this stage. High emotional intelligence will be vital during this stage, along with high engagement. What can you do to help with forming? One way is to be sure roles and responsibilities are clear.

Storming is another stage that the team will go through and is the most challenging. The players have been formed and told they are a team. However, there is still a lot of uncertainty about how they will get the work done during this stage. You did explain roles and responsibilities when they formed, but there is still uncertainty about how it all comes together. There may be conflict and resistance during this stage as they get to know each other and you. The team may question you as the leader, your style, and authority. Something that can also happen is that the team may become divided. Team members find out who is aligned with them and who may be outside their boundaries. Don't be afraid of this stage but be very aware of what is happening on the court and off the court. Storming is one of the scariest stages because if teams stay in this stage, they can be detrimental to the organization and you. It would be best to establish how (when forming) you and the team will deal with conflict and have honest conversations early in the process. This is particularly important so they don't get stuck in storming. Engagement is important during this stage, and listening will be critical. It is also imperative for you as the leader to be very present during this stage. The team may need you to step in at times. One of the biggest mistakes leaders make is leaving the team to figure it out independently. The team will stay in storming if you are not on the court with them.

Norming is when the team really comes together. Conflicts are resolved quickly, roles are clear, and a sense of mutual respect for you and others is within reach. Think about it as if things are normalizing and just an everyday part of their lives. The team feels more committed to the team goals, and they can give and receive feedback more effectively. This stage is where execution is prevalent. Projects are getting completed. Innovation is at its highest. Mistakes are normalized as just a part of the learning and developing process.

As the leader, you can allow the team to work without much guidance. The team is beginning to function independently so that you can focus on the bigger picture. However, keep in mind, if a project gets too complicated or complex, the team may go back to storming. That is okay! They have established some norms, and they can resolve conflicts much quicker and get back to norming or even catapult to high performing.

Performing is where you want to be. The team is working like a well-oiled machine. They are working effectively and efficiently on projects. They are synchronized and work easily together and with you. If differences occur or come up, they know how to navigate through for the good of the team and the organization. The team has a high degree of autonomy during this stage. The team is in full execution mode without the need for direction from the leader. They rely on each other to get the work done.

It's important to know that this team development model is not linear. Teams can go back and forth between the stages. It would be best to recognize where they are, and you can lead them through. If you recall, we spoke about meeting people where they are when you are building the relationship management muscle. For example, when you add a new team member, the team must go back to forming for a bit to allow for the new teammate to adjust.

Ponder these questions as you think about your team today.

- At what stage of team development do you think you should establish team norms?
- At what stage of team development would you be sure you have created a safe space for the team to interact?
- At what stage of team development could you help the team even more by creating team bonding opportunities?
- At what stage of team development would you have one on ones?
- At what stage of team development would you throw a pass? Give an assist? Put on a full-court press?

It is also valuable to note that going through the stages of team development can take time. However, it is also essential that the team not stay in any stage for an extended time. If a team stays in a particular stage for too long, that is a true indicator that something is going wrong. Maybe the norms aren't explicit, or there isn't a system in place to manage conflict, or there isn't enough communication. As the leader, it is your responsibility to recognize what is happening within your team and make the adjustments. You might even need to call a timeout.

Team building and developing team chemistry are vital to the team's success and organization. If you are looking for some team-building activities, check out the resources at the end of the book.

Bench strength is defined by the competence and number of employees ready to fill vacant positions. This is your sign to take a serious look at your current team members and all they bring to the team and the organization. It is a part of your role as a leader to prepare your team members for their next role on your team or within the organization. I know you may not want to hear this, but you could be preparing your team members to leave the organization. That is ok too. Great leaders/coaches develop their players/associates in the moment, and for the time they have them on their team. It would be egocentric for you to hold onto a person ready to move on.

How strong and competent is your bench? What can be done to increase their competence, so they are ready to get in the game, move up in the organization, or move on.

We all know you have that "go-to" player or players within your team, the one you want to take the last shot in the waning seconds, but what if you could count on others too? How are you building your bench strength to make that happen?

To build your bench strength and develop ALL the people on your team, contemplate these questions:

- Are you building up everyone on the team or just your high performers?
- Who are the ones just cheering for others to be successful? They may be comfortable just "cheering."
- What roles do people play on the team? Who are the current "Go-To" players?
- What can you do to develop others so that they can be "go-to" players?
- What skills do your team members need to grow and develop?

Talent is one small part of what it takes to build a successful basketball team, and the same goes for a team of employees in the workplace. Often, a team working together with a strong work ethic will trump a team that relies on individual talent alone. In sports and the business world, talent is important, but it can only take someone so far on its own.

"A player who makes the team great is better than a great player."

John Wooden

Recruit like a basketball coach. In the book, *Workquake: Embracing the Aftershocks of Covid-19 to Create a Better Model of Working* (Amplify Publishing) by Steve Cadigan, the message basketball recruiters send to prospects is: "If you come to my college, I will prepare you better than anyone else can for your future career." Cadigan says that "companies need to do the same thing."

In the past ten years, the median job tenure for professional employees dropped to 4.9 years from 5.2, according to the Bureau of Labor Statistics. This may not seem like a significant change, but that number is considerably lower for younger generations: For college graduates aged 25 to 34, the median tenure is just 2.8 years. It is simply unrealistic to expect an employee to stay at your company for twenty years. You'd be lucky if they stayed for five. So instead of making promises of long-term employment, tell applicants: "If you come here to work, you'll learn more in one year than you would anywhere else, and you'll meet people who can help catapult your career." Mold that talented person that you believed in when you hired them. Remember, you may be preparing them to move up or move on. When I was at Cornell, I had to "sell" the promise of an Ivy League education to compete for high-level players.

Cadigan concludes, "While they're working for you, help them build their skills and expand their professional networks, and when they move on to other opportunities, celebrate their departures. Turnover is healthy. It creates new opportunities for existing staff and allows new talent to come in and shake up ingrained habits, bringing innovative ideas and solutions to challenges."

Teach the fundamentals to everyone on the team. I recall a quote once used during my time at Cornell, "You are only as strong as your weakest link."

Practice humility. Humility leads to genuine collaboration, which is the cornerstone of any high-functioning team.

Tryouts:
Three Building Blocks

"My job is to do the work, and how many people watch it, the reception that it gets, and all of that is just business. My job is to go in, do the role and do the best job I can do. It doesn't matter whether you're on NBC, CBS, UPN, The WB, or whatever. It doesn't matter. Your job is to go in and do that job to the best of your ability every week."

Alfonso Ribeiro

Three Building Blocks

When an employee is first hired, the employee is put through a training program where they learn the ropes of the position and how to do the job well. This may be a structured training program or merely on-the-job training. At my company, the first 90 days is considered a probationary/training period. The new hire is being trained on how to perform the job functions and learning to see if the job is a right fit for them and the employer. As it is in basketball, **tryouts** are a **probationary/training period**. The coaching staff is trying to figure out if the player is a fit for the team. The coach may put the prospective player to the test in structured drills and game-play to see how the player performs. The coach looks at the skill level, ability, coachability, and many other aspects.

The **probationary/tryout period** begins with on-boarding. Unemployment is low right now, job openings are at an all-time high, and due to the Great Resignation, it is important to provide considerable opportunities to engage employees from day one. Creating a sound on-boarding process will provide your new employees with the early tools and knowledge they need for long-term success. It will aid them in assimilating and inserting themselves into your organization. It will increase your chances of retaining that valuable talent you've attracted. On-boarding programs are designed to educate and embed the company culture into a new hire while keeping them engaged. That way, they better understand their role in the organization, giving them a sense of belonging and directly affecting their loyalty.

What is your onboarding process? Is it effective? Is it comprehensive? Does it need to be revamped? Take time to evaluate your strategy today and make the necessary adjustments.

Next, let's introduce a few terms that may be valuable as you work through the tryout or probationary period with your team.

A Transition is the act of when possession of the ball changes. Thinking about leadership, it might be when you coach someone on reducing call talk time. As leaders, we may focus on how the player transitions from one aspect of the call to another. Or if they must make sales, how they transition into the sale depending on the call type. You can learn a lot about your player in how they perform during a transition.

The Scouting Report/Goals: Think about the **scouting report** as the road map for team success. Usually, a scouting report has information about your opposing team; yours still can if you want to "scout" your competition. Instead of looking at the players, look at the processes of your competitors and figure out ways to beat them.

A **scouting report**, just like your goals, shouldn't be written in stone; they are constantly changing as the game goes on. Same in business, you thought that the competition might change as the world changes, and so do the players. You may have to research your competition. Create a team scouting report about your competition. Think about a company, a competitor, who may have been bought out. How can you take advantage while they are making changes to compete? What are they doing well, and how do you measure up to that? You can use this activity of creating a scouting report as a development opportunity for one of your team members. Delegate researching the competition and use a scouting report template to report their findings at a team meeting. Learn about the competition and its players and their tendencies from your research, then ask how this information will help your team.

As you recognize what they are running, call it out to the rest of your team at the next team meeting and gather the team to garner ideas on how you can compete. One of the tools used as the first step in scouting is a **SWOT analysis**, which identifies strengths, weaknesses, opportunities, and threats. Business leaders use the SWOT tool to learn about their competition. Knowing your team's (and your competitions') Strengths, Weaknesses, Opportunities, and Threats can help leaders build their projects and processes more effectively.

Do a SWOT analysis on your team. What is the scouting report for your team? This report could be valuable to identify what you may need to do to improve the team.

"It's harder to stay on top than it is to make the climb. Continue to seek new goals."

Pat Summit

Goal Setting is the process of deciding what you want to accomplish and devising a plan to achieve those desired results. Goals can give you a clear focus, motivate employees, and set targets for your business to work towards. You will also want to set personal goals as a part of this process. When you walk onto a court to practice alone, you shouldn't just shoot around. Count your shots and put together personal objectives and goals for the practice time. This is goal setting.

It is vital to get buy-in from every team member to devise these goals. As a leader, you should not create the goals for the team in a bubble. You need input from the team because they are the ones who will be doing a lot of the executing. Executing is one of the aspects of the triple threat, so don't let it fail here. Not only will you have team goals, but each team member should have at least 3-5 goals that fit into the overall team and organizational goals. Books have been written about goal setting, so I will just introduce a few pointers on how essential goals are to you as a leader.

Goals are the foundation of the coaching conversations I have with my clients in my coaching business. We can think of goals in two ways, long-term and short-term. A **long-term goal** is something you want to accomplish in the future. **Long-term goals** require time and planning. They are not something you can do this week or possibly not even this year. **Long-term goals** are usually at least several years away. It takes many steps to complete a **long-term goal**. The smaller steps you take to achieve the long-term goal can be your short-term goals.

A **short-term goal** is something you want to do in the near future. The near future can mean today, this week, this month, or even this year. A **short-term goal** is something you want to accomplish soon.

An example of a **long-term goal** is to become a Chief Executive Officer at a Fortune 500 corporation by the time you are forty-five. Dream big, my friends! What will be your goals/plans to accomplish this in the short term?

- Identify and contact ten executives to network with over the year. Choose one person per month to contact and ask questions about how they prepared to become a CEO.

- Manage a three-month project from start to finish. Create the project scope, timelines, and milestones. Use a project scope template from a project management course.
- Attend the Leaders of America conference in May 2022 to increase my network by five executives, including a CFO and a CIO.
- What else could you add to this goal?

This is just a simple example of goal setting. I will simplify it even more.

 Be sure your goals are…
Specific
Actionable
Measurable

Think. Feel. Act.

Build the Brand:
Trust the Process

"Be more concerned with your character than your reputation because your character is what you really are, while your reputation is merely what others think you are."

John Wooden

Build the Brand

Building the Brand applies in basketball and business. Companies build up their brand to recognize it as a top product like the NBA/WNBA, Duke University, the Charlotte Hornets, American Express, Zappos, Mercedes, etc. These brands market themselves to build up their name to be recognized as one of the best. The same goes with how a program or an individual plays/ practices; their performances will resonate within the league/team on how intense they may be on defense or who will be the "go-to" person. As your team develops, so will the brand. In organizations where I have worked, I have heard people say, "I want to be on your team because I heard that you are fair, and you drive your employees to perform by supporting and coaching them. How do I get on your team?" I was building my brand as a leader.

Trust the process is another phrase used in the basketball and business world. A leader may not be upset by the win/loss record, more so upset over the efforts of individuals or the inability to run the offense/ defense as practiced. As the season wears on and they become more comfortable in the team game plan, they become more efficient. Trusting their game plan/

process would help the team reach their goals. Same in business, trust the process, invest in your people. I have used this before to show that there are many ways to get to the same answer/goal. What is 5+4? What is 8+1? What is 15 − 6? They all equal 9, which was only three ways to get there. Trust the process; we may not all get to the answer in the same way. Let that simmer for a minute.

In building your brand and your team, the players must perform. Whether we like it or not, you will have people on your team who just aren't quite up to the challenge. I often find myself referring to "all the way to the line" in my household/business (Kacee Reid). Many times, you hear coaches yell, "touch the line" or "all the way to the line." As a player, this has always baffled me. Why would someone go through all the effort to run down the court and back and not touch the line?! But this mentality holds true in life as well. So many of us will do 95% of the work or only give 95% time and effort not to finish the job. Finish as strong as you started. Someone will spend hours on a project and present amazing ideas in a work setting, but they misspell a simple word. They did 95% of the work but didn't "touch the line"! What would be a strategy you could use to inspire your team to "touch the line"? Are there players on your team who are only giving 95%? What can you do as the leader to raise accountability and raise the expectation to 100%?

As coaches and leaders, we can empower the more skilled players to work with their teammates who lack specific skills. For example, a very skilled shooter can help teach other players the shooting drills that helped them learn to shoot. Ask your excel guru to host a lunch and learn to share best practices or hold a workshop on excel tips and tricks.

Delegation is an essential skill for leaders to develop. Most of us have lived by the mantra, "if I want things to be done right, then I will do it myself" Well, you cannot do it all, and you shouldn't. By delegating, the head coach/leader will have the opportunity to work with a broader range of players. Allocation of authority also extends to other coaches/leaders on your staff. One sign of a great leader is their willingness to endorse others on their staff. Empowering others establishes trust and helps build a strong character for assistant coaches/managers/leaders and players.

The Off the Court Culture:
A Winning Culture

"Culture eats strategy for breakfast."

Peter Drucker

A Winning Culture

What we do off the court is just as critical as what we do on the court. As discussed earlier in the On the Court chapter, a team cannot accomplish the goals if the off-court behaviors are not aligned with the on-court behavior. Influential leaders collaborate across the boundaries, outside of the 94'x 50', before you step on the court. A leader in athletics once said to us – "as student-athletes, you live in a glasshouse. People can see what you are doing all the time." We must be keenly aware of the image we portray at all times. This is true in leadership as well. What kind of team atmosphere are you depicting? Are you providing a culturally safe space off the court as well?

Should you, as the leader, provide a safe space for honesty, humility, and healthy dialogue in the space in which you work? Good coaches/leaders of teams should never resort to belittlement, manipulation, or force. It is a part of your responsibility as a leader to create a safe and trusting team atmosphere. There is no place for any type of abusive language or behavior. Whether a leader on the court or in the office – you're a role model – so act like one!

Crucial basketball moments don't just happen with

time winding down on the clock. They happen all the time during practice, during the first quarter, and in the clutch. They also occur off the court, so good basketball players, like a good leader anywhere, need to constantly monitor their behavior because of the trickle-down impact on others around them.

Most of the work is done off the court or in your office and outside the team space. This is where you behave in honor of the mission and the vision. A team cannot accomplish the goals if the off-court behaviors are not aligned with the on-court behavior. In thinking about the off-court safe space:

- Are you an inclusive leader?
- Do you make visible commitments to diversity, hold others accountable for their behaviors?
- Do you make Diversity, Equity, and Inclusion a personal priority?
- Do you show humility by admitting mistakes and making a safe space for others to contribute?
- Do you have a keen awareness of bias, conscious and unconscious?
- Do you recognize your blind spots when it comes to diversity?
- Do you see flaws in the system and speak out?
- Do you lead with an open mindset, listen

without judgment, and seek understanding
with empathy?
- Do you possess cultural intelligence by
being attentive to others' cultures?

Cultural Safety

I would be remiss if I didn't address the concept of cultural safety. It is a vital part of any high-performing team. As leaders, we can influence this notion within our teams and organizations. This concept of cultural safety can be applied to people of different faith groups, ethnicities, cultures, sexual orientations, and gender expression.

An unsafe cultural space is where actions can demean or exclude individuals based on their cultural identity. An unsafe environment can also be used to justify or rationalize certain behaviors. This can take the form of jokes about sexual orientation or other offensive jokes. This type of behavior is not OK. It can also take the form of cliques that exclude people based on their race or ethnicity.

Teams that focus on cultural safety establish deep-rooted levels of trust, making them highly successful. A few ways to promote cultural safety on your team are to:

- Develop a list of team values that are linked to appropriate behavior. These can be used to guide discussions about team culture and behavior. These can be different than your team norms.

- Hold biweekly team meetings designed to build connections and discuss common concerns.
- Create engagement opportunities for connection around culture. Bring in culturally diverse foods as a lunch option for the team to experience.
- Normalize conflict and don't be afraid of it. People make mistakes. Simply manage awkward cultural situations so they don't create distress and sidetrack your team.
- Make cultural safety part of your team norms in a way that feels good for ALL on the team.

We are going to **transition** into putting it all together. In the next section, Overtime, you will find leader scenarios where you can create your own Xs and Os to lead through the language of basketball.

What stage of team development
is your team in today? Forming?
Storming? Norming? Performing?

What can you do to move your team
to the next stage?

What is your brand? How do you
know it is apparent to others?

How are you tracking on your short
terms goals this month?

How can you strengthen your bench
this month? Be specific

Team Development

Julia Weaver

The Next Stage

Julia Weaver

Your Brand

_____

_____

_____

_____

_____

_____

_____

_____

_____

_____

_____

_____

_____

_____

Tracking Short
Term Goals

_____

_____

_____

_____

_____

_____

_____

_____

_____

_____

_____

_____

_____

_____

Julia Weaver

Strengthening
Your Bench

Julia Weaver

Overtime

"Most people get excited about games, but I've got to be excited about practice because that's my classroom."

Pat Summit

Overtime

Skill development begins with deliberate practice. Practices consistent of activities explicitly intended to improve performance by reaching objectives just beyond the individual's level of competence. If you want to be a leader, you must practice. You will only get better the more you practice. Do something repeatedly to gain new insights and constantly improve. You wouldn't play a game without practicing, so practice your shot, your passing, and your dribbling. Get in the triple threat position, and let's go!

Exercise 1
Leader Scenarios

Think through each of these scenarios and make notes on how you would handle each situation. Use the terms and the common language that has been introduced throughout the entirety of this book.

- An employee comes to you with a suggestion to help the team. You think it is an innovative idea.

- An employee in a long meeting asks a tough question. They question the value of the project you're all focused on. "How did we get here? What made us decide to do this in the first place?" Shocked and offended, you think to yourself, "How dare they question my decision?"

- You have someone on your team in a role you've never done yourself. You're not familiar with all the nuances of what they do, nor their keys to success.

- Morale is low; what can you do to build team spirit?

- It's near the end of the month, and you haven't met your financial goals.

- Your company is recruiting from outside your region. You were raised in an area where everyone says things indirectly and gently, but your new hire is more direct. You are holding a team meeting to discuss a new project, and this new hire has lots of ideas.

- You hire a coach to help you be a better leader. The coach encourages you passionately to do something you've never gotten around to doing yet.

- You have been placed in charge of a project team for a new project. What are your first steps to get the team going and complete the project?

- You have an employee who is constantly pushing your boundaries.

- You have a team member that continues to make the same mistake repeatedly.

- A team member you've invested a lot of time and energy in mentoring decides to leave?

- You take a hard look at your team, and all your "go-to" team members all look like you.

- You just started in a new position with new direct reports; what do you do first?

- Your new team is dabbling in remote work; how do you set the expectations for how work will get done and how the team will communicate?

Exercise 2
Leader Scenarios in Overtime

You will need extra time to work through these more complex scenarios.

- Three members of your team, Lori, Conner, and Keyshawn, are working on a project that needs to be done in time for an 8 am meeting tomorrow. Lori is overtime-eligible, Keyshawn (a high performer) and Conner (a moderate performance) are overtime-exempt. It is close to 5 pm when the three usually leave the office for the day (they all work 8 - 5). The project is not yet complete. How do you handle this situation? What skills will you use?

- Vince has been missing a significant amount of work for various reasons (sick leave, car broke down, helping parents, etc.). In a team meeting, Belinda comments on everyone pulling their weight. Vince becomes upset and begins shouting, Vince and Belinda are your direct reports.

- Tan, your employee, overhears an inappropriate conversation between Lonzo and Denise, two coworkers from your colleague Winston's team. Tan reports to you that she overheard racial or ethnic references in the exchange directed at Kai, another employee on your team. How will you handle this situation?

• As a supervisor, you've made an unpopular decision. What action would you take, so that morale in the department is not negatively affected?

Exercise 3

One of the concepts of the triple threat is Engagement. Here are some ideas on how you can drive engagement and build trust.

Fifteen Days of Engagement
• **Day 1** – Ask a team member each week to create an activity or game using Kahoot, Menti, or other engagement tools.
• **Day 2** – Identify someone on the team for being a team player; what did they do, and how did it impact the team?
• **Day 3** – Enhance your active listening skills, clarify what you heard by repeating back to the speaker.
• **Day 4** – Make a chest pass to one of your team members today – remember the chest pass is one that people can catch.

- **Day 5** – Show your appreciation for two teammates today. Be specific about what they have done that has impacted the team.
- **Day 6** – Create a fast break opportunity today.
- **Day 7** – Only use the word "we" today when describing anything happening on the team
- **Day 8** - Who from your team inspires you, and how do they do that? Let them know publicly.
- **Day 9** – Update the team on an organizational goal or milestone.
- **Day 10** – Give employees an extra 15-30 minutes this week to do something active or for wellness such as yoga, stretching, walking, etc.
- **Day 11** – Host an "out of the box" brainstorming session to welcome team goals or engagement ideas.
- **Day 12** – Find out what day today is – National Doughnut Day or National Hot Dog Day – then ask about favorite doughnut flavors or what toppings people like on their hot dog/carrot dog.
- **Day 13** – Create a monthly lunch and learn – 15-minute session on diverse topics – create a task force or person in charge – Can this be a stretch assignment for players on the team? Would this opportunity develop them into a 'go-to" player?
- **Day 14** – Once a month, have your cameras on for the team meeting and have Dress Up Day, Sunglasses Day, Fancy Hat, Black Tie, or Band T-Shirt Day.
- **Day 15** – Create a word cloud with the first name of each teammate or the name of your team, or the department you represent. Use words that

define your mission, vision, or for the person. Use encouraging/positive words about that person and the characteristics you admire.

Bonus idea – Buy Hoopspeak for your leadership team and create a book club, so you all are creating your team language. Or buy any other leadership book or team development book and start connecting with conversations and ideas to build your team and leadership skills.

What will you Start doing? Stop doing? Continue doing?

Start? Stop? Continue?

_____

_____

_____

_____

_____

_____

_____

_____

_____

_____

_____

_____

_____

_____

_____

Write down eight skills that you enjoy doing frequently.

Write down eight skills that you do frequently yet find draining.

Favorite Skills

1. _____

2. _____

3. _____

4. _____

5. _____

6. _____

7. _____

8. _____

Draining Skills

1. _____

2. _____

3. _____

4. _____

5. _____

6. _____

7. _____

8. _____

Visit your values. Are they currently aligning with your work?

Choose one of the fifteen ways to engage your team this week. Write about how it influenced you, the team, or the organization.

Values

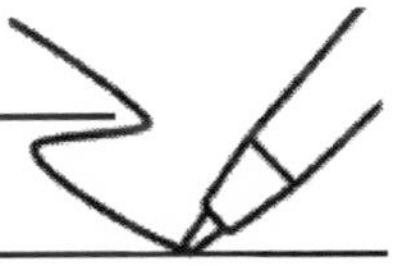

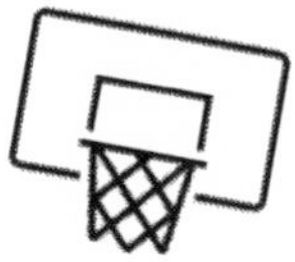

Engage

Julia Weaver

Conclusion

*"At the end of the game, the king
and the pawn go back in the same box"*

Italian proverb

Conclusion

The quote, for me, means that we are all in this together. While the King may have a "title" and higher rank, you still need the pawn (the team members/players) to play the game. You've just finished reading this book, and your head is swimming with ideas. You're probably wondering, where do I begin? At the end of the day, the month, or the year, are you going to be 1-0 or 0-1? What does that indeed mean? Mostly, it tells how are you going to measure your day, your month, or your year? Are you experiencing more wins than losses in the game of leading?

It will be important for you to track those wins. Throughout Hoopspeak, there have been many questions posed to you to ponder and respond. Take time to answer those questions as you continue to develop your philosophy and become the leader you chose to be.

Basketball games have the unique ability to raise people and fans to emotional highs. Work can do that for you too. So, while you are at work or in work mode, be nervous, enjoy the fact that you have a team, and a challenge to overcome with people who care if you succeed or fail. We all have crucial moments in the day-to-day. Take some time to think about how you want to behave the next time you shoot a brick at work, and when you do, we all have; how do you respond?

Give thanks to those people who have the courage to help you learn by pointing out your missteps or blunders and who challenge you to elevate your game to a higher level. Never forget from where you came. Pay homage to all your past teachers, coaches, and leaders. Acknowledge others in the organization or in your daily life that aren't necessarily on your team, like the barista who knows your name and how you take your coffee, the maintenance person who ensures you have a working overhead light, the staff that keeps the offices clean and sanitary and foremost the support staff who keep you organized and equipped for the game.

I will admit, at one time, I wanted to be like my mentor, my coach, and my friend Lynne Agee but the hard truth she said to me was that I couldn't be like her. I had to be me. I couldn't be her; she was already taken. I have so much respect for her saying that to me.

Stay humble. Learn from your losses, your failures, and all the missteps. They will happen. Do you recall that I challenged you to normalize mistakes? We all make them. Learn from jobs not gotten. Learn from others. Be gentle with yourself, especially on tough days. Whatever you do, make a decision, and go hard. Sprint when you need to and apply the full-court press.

Always be sure you "touch the line."

It doesn't matter what the coach/leader knows if they can't teach the players. It doesn't matter how great your offense is if the players can't catch the pass, find the open player/associate, and hit the open shots. Spend time on the fundamentals every day.

Join LinkedIn and other communities of leaders and coaches. The best decision I ever made was joining a community of coaches when I received my professional coach certification through the Fowler International Academy. We meet each week to share best practices, wins, losses, and most importantly, we support each other. Coaches and leaders need coaches.

In drawing to a close, I would like to share a final example of using the language of basketball to strategize and turn around a unit within an organization. My friend Bill offered this extraordinary story (Hoopspeak) of how he led using Xs and Os and the common language of basketball:

As a mid-level leader within the Central Intelligence Agency for an engineering organization (Development & Maintenance), I had the opportunity to apply for an operational leadership assignment. I didn't have prior operational experience; however, I built a name for myself across the Information Operation Center (IOC) for turning a struggling unit into a relevant, productive organization. I remember the conversation with my boss about the new opportunity. In his opinion, he supported my candidacy for the position but looked for me to dismantle/shut down the operational organization if I were to get the position. I challenged him on the guidance.

If given a chance to lead the operational organization, I needed the chance to turn things around (*pivot*). I wasn't interested in the position if my sole objective was to shut down the organization. He agreed. I applied for the job and was selected to lead the operational mission. I knew the challenge was analogous to taking a *3-point shot* in basketball – especially given my ability to play basketball. I knew the odds were against me. But I wanted to take the *shot*. I was willing to give it my best to help a struggling organization get back into the game.

Honestly, my boss had an excellent argument for shutting things down because there were a lot of issues (*SWOT*). The personnel in the operational unit were good officers, but there were lapses in policy, process, and procedural adherence to programmatic and operational practices. A few months into the assignment, I determined it was one of the toughest jobs but most rewarding. For example, rebuilding a struggling organization requires tough decisions. In my opinion, it's easier to stand up a new initiative (fun also) or to lead a successful team. I found it extremely difficult (a skill not often taught) to terminate projects or cancel operations. Making tough decisions or changing the status quo often leads to personnel leaving the team because they don't share the new vision. Similarly, asking personnel to leave the team to find other opportunities is equally taxing.

Rebuilding a team is stressful. The *turnover* affects the performance and morale of the overall team, and it takes time to recruit talent and rebuild a successful team. As a leader, you cannot expect a 'win' overnight (*forming, storming, norming, and performing*). It takes time to *recruit* talent and rebuild your organizational playbook. Regardless, the time clock continues to tick, and your leadership expects results. The *timeouts* are limited. I discovered the need to prioritize which programs and operations were the most productive and the least productive. I give my boss credit for giving me sufficient time to make the changes, support the changes, and realize that progress can also be measured by stopping efforts that don't contribute to the team's success. Ultimately, it will free up resources to redirect elsewhere. I recruited talented personnel to lead various programmatic and operational efforts.

My leadership team and I slowly began to turn things around for the mission. My peers and my senior leadership within the IOC started to take notice. Personally, my epiphany occurred when an exceptionally talented person knocked on my door and asked to join the leadership team — we were becoming the team to join, *building the brand!* After taking a new assignment, I used my experience to mentor others. It was personally rewarding to watch my leadership team, and I rebuild the mission to continue their successful record. In my opinion, some of the toughest jobs, *long-shots,* are the most rewarding, but you need to be prepared for the mental and emotional capital it takes. More importantly, you need to take the tough assignments for the right reasons – because you want to make a difference!

This is your journey. Use all the tools you have at your disposal, especially the language of basketball, to guide you along the way. With all, you have learned and all you already know, go out and carve your leader path. I want you to be successful. If you genuinely want to increase your emotional intelligence, give me a chance to help you. If you're going to raise your self-awareness, let me assist. I want to support you in your leadership journey. I would love to hear from you. Email me your wins and your losses. I wholeheartedly believe that we learn just as much or more from our failures and losses as we do from the wins.

"A failure isn't a failure if it prepares you for success tomorrow."

Lolo Jones

If you want a coach, contact me, and let's take a journey of self-discovery together. I can help you set goals, and together, we can get there. We can rack up more wins than losses, and you can feel great about your winning record as a leader.

Think. Feel. Act.

Thoughts? Feelings? Actions?

Who can you enhance a relationship
with this week; a teammate, peer,
colleague, or client?

What tools will you use?

Thoughts? Feelings? Actions?

Who can you enhance a relationship with this week; a teammate, peer, colleague, or client?
What tools will you use?

_____

_____

_____

_____

_____

_____

_____

_____

_____

_____

_____

_____

How are the off-court behaviors aligning with the on-court behaviors within your team?

How did you provide a safe space for people on your team this month?

Off-court Behaviors
On-court Behaviors

Julia Weaver

Safe Space

Who can you give an assist
to today? What project or task will
you delegate?

When can you expect it to be
completed? How will you support
the team member?

Assist? Delegate? Support?

_____

_____

_____

_____

_____

_____

_____

_____

_____

_____

_____

_____

_____

_____

How will you execute this week?

Can you identify any reasons
why you may need to apply
a full-court press?

What is the situation?

Execute

Incorporate three of the
foundational terms in your
interactions this week.
Craft your plan here.

Plans

_____

_____

_____

_____

_____

_____

_____

_____

_____

_____

_____

_____

_____

_____

_____

Biography

Julia A. Weaver is a veteran coach and skilled facilitator. Along with her MSEd, Julia is a Certified Professional Coach, a Certified YouMap® Coach, a Certified Executive Leadership Coach, and a certified Disaster Recovery Coach. Beginning her career as a Division I college basketball coach, she started to hone her coaching muscle. In every position she has held, she has been able to weave coaching throughout every interaction. She has considerable experience in a wide variety of disciplines. Julia has worked in the education world, the non-profit sector, retail, healthcare, telecommunications, consulting, and entrepreneurship.

Julia prides herself in her ability to listen and ask the "right" questions! Through the questions, she can guide

YOU on YOUR journey to discover the best in you. She can help you identify and create goals, and she is the ultimate supporter. She will serve as your accountability partner. Everyone needs one of those. Even coaches need coaches. Julia uses a holistic, intuitive tool called YouMap® tool for Career and Personal Exploration in her coaching business. For more information about YouMap®, you will find it here, www.myyoumap.com. Send Julia an email (Julia@weaversp.com) to set up for an initial self-discovery call. You won't regret sending that email.

Julia is also available to facilitate a cadre of courses for your organization. All she needs is a time slot and the materials. Courses, workshops, and topics she has experience delivering include Leading a Multi-Generational Workforce, Diversity, Equity and Inclusion initiatives, Leader Development, Change Management, Emotional Intelligence, Empathy, Values, Trust, and even systems training such as Salesforce. She is available as a facilitator to deliver virtual courses using multiple platforms such as Microsoft TEAMS, Adobe Connect, WebEx, and Zoom. Julia will also serve on your organizational panels to discuss many topics.

Julia and her partner enjoy exploring small towns, relaxing on any body of water, and grilling. Their two cats, Georgia and Lola, live a life of luxury, and they don't mind spoiling them.

Contact Julia: julia@weaversp.com
Website: www.weaverstrategicpartners.com

Follow Julia on social media!

Facebook: HoopspeakXandO
Instagram: HoopspeakXandO
Twitter: @HoopspeakXandO
Tik Tok: @jweaverllc
YouTube: Hoopspeak
Snapchat: Julia_weaver13
LinkedIn: Julia Weaver

Resources

Books:

Brown, Brené (2016) *Dare to Lead: Brave Work. Tough Conversations. Whole Hearts.* Random House.

Bungay Stanier, Michael. (2016) *The Coaching Habit: Say Less, Ask More & Change the Way You Lead Forever.* Box of Crayons Press.

Cadigan, Steve. (2021) *Workquake: Embracing the Aftershocks of Covid-19 to Create a Better Model of Working.* Amplify Publishing.

Lencioni, Patrick. (2002) *The Five Dysfunctions of a Team: A Leadership Fable.* Jossey-Bass.

Loehr, Jim and Tony Schwartz. (2003) T*he Power of Full Engagement.* Free Press.

Pink, Daniel H. (2017) *Drive: The Surprising Truth About What Motivates Us.* Riverhead Books.

Salerno, Ann and Lillie Brock (2008) *The Change Cycle: How People Can Survive and Thrive in Organizational Change.* Berrett-Koehler Publishers.

Scott, Kim. (2017) *Radical Candor: Be a Kick-Ass Boss Without Losing Your Humility.* St. Martin's Press.

Scott, Susan. (2017) *Fierce Conversations: Achieving Success at Work and Life One Conversation at a Time, Reprint edition.* Berkley.

Sherry, Kristin A. (2021) *Maximize 365: A Year of Actionable Tips to Transform Your Life.* Black Rose Writing.
(2020) *Your Team Loves Mondays, Right? A Guide for People Managers.* Black Rose Writing.
(2018) *YouMap: Find Yourself. Blaze Your Path. Show the World! Second Edition.* Black Rose Writing.

Sinek, Simon. (2014) *Leaders Eat Last: Why Some Teams Pull Together, and Others Don't.* Portfolio.

Development offerings:

Engagement Starts with Your Leaders: Create a Culture of High Energy and Commitment Through the 4 Levels of Leadership. Tom Roth, Wilson Learning https://www.wilsonlearning.com/wlw/articles/l/engagement-leaders/en

Why Trust Is Critical to Team Success (n.d.) The Center for Creative Leadership. https://www.ccl.org/articles/white-papers/trust-critical-team-success/

Focus on 3 Needs to Improve Team Performance (n.d.) The Center for Creative Leadership. https://www.ccl.org/articles/leading-effectively-articles/what-does-your-team-need/

TEDTalk presenters:

Brené Brown
Simon Sinek

Websites and useful links:

- Inc.com
- Harvard Business Review
- HR.com
- Forbes.com
- Basketball
- bkbfoundation.com

Ohman, Kyle. "The Value of Communication in Basketball" (n.d.) *Basketball.*
    https://basketballhq.com/the-value-of-communication-in-basketball

"The Complete Team Basketball Defensive Game Plan" (n.d.) *Basketball.*
    https://basketballhq.com/the-complete-team-basketball-defensive-game-plan

Basketball. "Help Recover and Baseline Drive Rotations Shell Drill" (n.d.)
> https://basketballhq.com/help-recover-and-baseline-drive-rotations-shell-drill

Basketball knowledge:

MiMi: Zone. Defense. Basketball. (n.d.)
> https://en.mimi.hu/basketball/zone_defense.html#maintitle

SPORTS LINGO: A DICTIONARY FOR COMMON SPORTS SLANG & JARGON (n.d.)
> https://www.sportslingo.com/sports-glossary/k/key/

What Is a Flagrant Foul in Basketball? A Complete Guide (n.d.) CoachingKidz.
> https://coachingkidz.com/flagrant-foul/?web=1&wdLOR=c8024C6C8-A333-40CC-8D5A-7ECE1BB8ADA5

Career building:

8 Myths about vulnerability that you need to know (n.d.) *My Question Life.*
> https://myquestionlife.com/myths-about-vulnerability/

EMPLOYEE TENURE IN 2020 Bureau of Labor Statistics. Department of Labor. (22 Sept. 2020). https://www.bls.gov/news.release/pdf/tenure.pdf

What is a Short-Term Goal? (n.d.) *My MN Careers.* https://careerwise.minnstate.edu/mymncareers/english-learner/short-term-goal.html

Connolly, Maria. *How to Be Courageous Enough to Set Strong Emotional Boundaries"* (n.d.) New Ways Center. http://newayscenter.com/2018/01/17/set-emotional-boundaries/

Quotations:

https://www.brainyquote.com/authors/sebastian-coe-quotes
Sebastian Coe

https://www.quotemaster.org/q3a3414a76fd20dbac89191db70172f50tp
Michael Jordan

https://www.searchquotes.com/quotes/author/Alfonso_Ribeiro/
Alfonso Ribeiro

Team building activities that will make an impact on team development:

- Helium stick activity to build team communication, discuss the importance of planning and encourage teamwork, leaders may emerge **https://team-building.org/helium-stick-team-building-game/**

(This activity is one of my personal favorites)

- Stepping Stones will focus on leadership skills, communication, planning, and working together as a team to accomplish the task **https://paradigmshiftleadership.com/stepping-stones-a-classic-group-collaboration-activity/**

- Human Knot will help the team learn to work together (close contact activity) **https://ventureteambuilding.co.uk/human-knot/**

- Traffic Jam activity for the team to combine their physical skills with group problem solving and cooperation skills **https://ventureteambuilding.co.uk/traffic_**

jam_team_building/
- Paper towers/Straw towers activity to get your team to think strategically

https://ventureteambuilding.co.uk/paper-tower/

- Egg Drop activity involves collaboration, problem-solving, and creative teamwork

https://www.freshtracks.co.uk/free-team-building/free-team-building-activity-egg-drop/

- Escape Rooms – Find local Escape Rooms for team problem solving

Scavenger Hunts - https://www.goosechase.com/blog/team-building-scavenger-hunt-ideas-for-the-office/

- Ice Breakers – Use to start meetings, energize the team, and get to know each other better

https://www.zoomshift.com/blog/icebreaker-games/

Made in the USA
Middletown, DE
18 March 2022

62837849R00139